SHIENA LENÉ

The Heart of The Matter Volume One

Prayers From Our Hearts to God's Ears

First published by SL Media 2018

Copyright © 2018 by Shiena Lené

All rights reserved. No part of this publication may be reproduced, stored or transmitted in any form or by any means, electronic, mechanical, photocopying, recording, scanning, or otherwise without written permission from the publisher. It is illegal to copy this book, post it to a website, or distribute it by any other means without permission.

Shiena Lené asserts the moral right to be identified as the author of this work.

Shiena Lené has no responsibility for the persistence or accuracy of URLs for external or third-party Internet Websites referred to in this publication and does not guarantee that any content on such Websites is, or will remain, accurate or appropriate.

Designations used by companies to distinguish their products are often claimed as trademarks. All brand names and product names used in this book and on its cover are trade names, service marks, trademarks and registered trademarks of their respective owners. The publishers and the book are not associated with any product or vendor mentioned in this book. None of the companies referenced within the book have endorsed the book.

Scripture quotations marked NLT are taken from the Holy Bible, New Living Translation, copyright © 1996, 2004, 2015 by Tyndale House Foundation. Used by permission of Tyndale House Publishers, Inc., Carol Stream, Illinois 60188. All rights reserved.

Scripture quotations marked TPT are from The Passion Translation®. Copyright © 2017, 2018 by Passion & Fire Ministries, Inc. Used by permission. All rights reserved. ThePassionTranslation.com.

First edition

Cover art by Gregory Johnson
Editing by Jean Dancy

This book was professionally typeset on Reedsy.
Find out more at reedsy.com

Dedicated to...YOU.

So it is with your prayers. Ask and you'll receive. Seek and you'll discover. Knock on heaven's door, and it will one day open for you. Every persistent person will get what he asks for. Every persistent seeker will discover what he needs. And everyone who knocks persistently will one day find an open door.

Luke 11:9-10 (TPT)

Contents

Preface   vii
Acknowledgement   ix

I   HEALING

1. WHEN SOMEONE YOU LOVE HAS HURT YOU   3
2. SCRIPTURES   4
3. OVERCOMING DEPRESSION   5
4. SCRIPTURES   7
5. GENERAL PHYSICAL HEALING   9
6. SCRIPTURES   11
7. DIGESTIVE SYSTEM   12
8. SCRIPTURES   13
9. BODY, SOUL & SPIRIT   14
10. SCRIPTURES   16

II   TRAVEL

11. DIVINE INTERFERENCE WITH TRAVEL   19
12. SCRIPTURES   20

III FINANCES

13	FINANCIAL RELEASE	25
14	SCRIPTURES	26

IV DESTINY & PURPOSE

15	KEEPING THE EGO SURRENDERED	29
16	SCRIPTURES	31
17	TRUSTING GOD IN SILENT MOMENTS	32
18	SCRIPTURES	33
19	REMEMBERING YOUR PURPOSE AND DESTINY	34
20	SCRIPTURES	35
21	MANIFESTING DREAMS	36
22	SCRIPTURES	37
23	PERSEVERE THROUGH THE PROCESS	38
24	SCRIPTURES	40
25	KEEPING DREAMS AT THE FEET OF GOD	42
26	SCRIPTURES	44
27	VICTORY	46
28	SCRIPTURES	47
29	BEING PURIFIED FOR PURPOSE	48
30	SCRIPTURES	49
31	SURRENDERING GOD'S PROMISE	50
32	SCRIPTURES	52

V ENCOURAGEMENT

33	WHEN YOU ARE WEARY	57
34	SCRIPTURES	59
35	GOD'S GLORY BE REVEALED	61

| 36 | SCRIPTURES | 62 |

VI ENDURANCE

37	TO ENDURE GROWING PAINS	67
38	SCRIPTURES	68
39	ENDURING DESPITE EMOTIONS	69
40	SCRIPTURES	70
41	WHEN FEELING OVERWHELMED	71
42	SCRIPTURES	72
43	PEACE OF MIND	73
44	SCRIPTURES	74

VII DIRECTION

45	HELP WITH MAKING DECISIONS	77
46	SCRIPTURES	78
47	FOR SURE DIRECTION	79
48	SCRIPTURES	80

VIII RESOLVING CONFLICT

49	WHERE TENSION IS OR MAY BE PRESENT	83
50	SCRIPTURES	84
51	WHEN SURROUNDED BY ENEMIES	85
52	SCRIPTURES	86
53	WHEN ENEMIES ARE STUBBORN	87
54	SCRIPTURES	88
55	WHEN HOLDING ONTO OFFENSE	90
56	SCRIPTURES	91
57	FORGIVENESS	92

58	SCRIPTURES	93
59	WHEN FACING TEMPTATION	95
60	SCRIPTURES	97
61	JEALOUSY	98
62	SCRIPTURES	99
63	FOR DECEPTION TO BE REVEALED	100
64	SCRIPTURES	101

IX FAMILY

65	PARENTING/LEGACY	105
66	SCRIPTURES	107
67	HOPE FOR SINGLE PARENTS	108
68	SCRIPTURES	110
69	WHEN FEELNG MISUNDERSTOOD	112
70	SCRIPTURES	113
71	FATHERS WHO ARE SEPARATED FROM THEIR CHILDREN	114
72	SCRIPTURES	116
73	CONCERNING BARRENNESS	117
74	SCRIPTURES	118
75	FOR BARREN WOMEN TO PRAY OVER THEMSELVES	119
76	SCRIPTURES	120
77	PREGNANCY AND LABOR	122
78	SCRIPTURES	124

X RELATIONSHIPS & MARRIAGE

79	WHEN A LOVED ONE HAS TRANSITIONED	129
80	SCRIPTURES	130
81	GETTING THROUGH GRIEF	131

82	SCRIPTURES	132
83	FREEDOM FROM TOXIC SOUL TIES	134
84	SCRIPTURES	135
85	TRUSTING COMPLETELY AND LOVING UNCONDITIONALLY	136
86	SCRIPTURES	137
87	GRACE TO LOVE UNCONDITIONALLY	138
88	SCRIPTURES	139
89	FOR A TROUBLED MARRIAGE	141
90	SCRIPTURES	142
91	DIVINE MARRIAGES	144
92	SCRIPTURES	146

XI TALENTS/GIFTS/BUSINESS ENDEAVORS

93	CREATIVE POWER AND GIFTS	151
94	SCRIPTURES	152
95	FAVOR IN BUSINESS AND INFLUENCE IN CITY	153
96	SCRIPTURES	155
97	FOR CREATIVES	156
98	SCRIPTURES	158
99	PRAYER FOR THE PRESIDENT OF THE UNITED STATE/UNITED STATES	160
100	SCRIPTURES	161

XII DECREE OVER YOURSELF

101	DAILY DECREE	165

XIII WHAT I BELIEVE

102	STATEMENT OF FAITH	169
103	TEACHERS I LOVE	171
104	PRAYER OF SALVATION	172
105	SCRIPTURES	173
106	PRAYER TO BREAK DEMONIC COVENANTS AND CURSES	174
107	SCRIPTURES	176
108	WORSHIP MUSIC I LOVE	177
109	PRAYER TO RECEIVE BAPTISM OF HOLY SPIRIT	178
110	SCRIPTURES	180

About the Author 182

Preface

This book is a collection of prayers that Father placed in my heart to share with you. Quick, full of truth and belief; rooted in unconditional love. Some of them are from my personal prayer time and most are prayers Father gave me, just for you.

While walking out my relationship with God I've realized when I'm solely focused on my emotions in prayer, I become a clouded vessel in that moment. Praying from an emotional space turns into a venting session without a solution. I have learned that prayers are most effective when spoken from a place of pure truth and a knowing of who I am in Jesus Christ. I encourage this posture tremendously when praying, because it essentially keeps motives selfless and our spirits open to hear clearly.

Religious ideals can portray prayer to be very mystifying sometimes, however during my journey with Father God I've realized how simple and practical prayer really is! Prayer is literally intentional conversation with Father. The best conversations I experience are the ones fueled with vulnerability. Vulnerability can be so uncomfortable but it's especially the best way to be with Father. I'm here to help you become more vulnerable in prayer. Being vulnerable with an attitude of gratefulness keeps the ego from becoming the culprit of destiny sabotage.

God's written word (2 Corinthians 12:9) says in our weakness He is the strongest within us. What a great formula for prayer! When we are vulnerable our ego is weak and humility rises up! THAT'S when we are standing tall in our true sense of self before Father. Children asking parents for what they need or simply saying thank you...fearlessly.

Sometimes prayers are comical and sassy or fervent and steadfast. Sometimes they're therapeutic and healing. All in all, the most important thing when praying is sincerity and an humble ear. Holy Spirit dwells within us and since our steps are ordered by Father, He knows exactly what we should pray (Psalm 37:23, Romans 8:26). As we grow in communion with Him, prayer becomes this beautiful rhythm with a lyrical song for every occasion. It's the perfect soundtrack to life!

Let these following prayers be a mere starting point for you. I believe as your confidence in your Christ identity grows, your prayers will become more confident. So be big and bold when you go before the King; He's the master of the Universe and He's also your friend. Take a moment after you have spoken to just listen. This is the most important part of prayer; listening for Father God's response. Again prayer is a conversation, so let Him freely speak! Be assured that Father has something to say specifically to you, and the heart of the matter.

Grace & Peace,

Shiena Lené

Acknowledgement

Thank you to my biological father, Dr. Robert C. Sneed, who instilled in me the importance of cultivating a personal relationship with God. I remember being 11 years old and him sharing with me to read my Bible everyday, and have a concordance so I could really study for understanding, then spend time in prayer. That routine became my spiritual regimen when I came home from school. That time in my life deeply anchored me to pursue the truth of who God is, and thirst for His presence in my personal walk. Thank you Dad!! Who knew those beginning days of prayer, would lead to me becoming an intercessor and author?

My Godfather Jeffery McClendon: You introduced me to the supernatural and you love me like I'm your own. I appreciate being able to call you with my crazy faith and you just encourage me to stand strong in my expectation for the miraculous. The way you believe in me always puts a smile on my face. Thank you Dad, I love you!

I'm so grateful for my spiritual father, Eddie Lee Long. I miss you tremendously and those Poppa Bear hugs! I was freed from the chains of religion and introduced to the true Kingdom of God through your teachings. My days of serving in ministry developed me for greatness, that I didn't even know I was capable of achieving. I am proudly carrying the baton that you well prepared me to catch.

Thank you Yarisette and Dionny Baez for allowing me to serve you and your vision. !Dios Mío! I am forever grateful! I love you two and your family forever (Milky! En nombre de Jesus, hermaña!!!).

Rhonda and Earlie James: you are answered prayer. Yes, I know- I'm stuck with you! :) Thank you for your support and keeping watch over me.

Kristi Wheeler: Your prayers really kept me. Thank for the time that you covered me. I appreciate you.

My prayer partner and the one whom I call Mom: Preness Marks. Do we have testimonies, or what? But there's so many more to come!!! God connected us and it's forever!! Thank you for being patient with me.

Motheren: Sandra 'Momma' Campbell. I remember when I called you and shared that it was in my spirit to cover a group of musicians in prayer, as well as just intercede together. You woke up with me every week and we PRAYED. I love you and have such a special place for you and your family in my heart. You will never truly know how much you all have made the difference in pivotal moments of my life. However, I CAN attempt to explain over food, cooked by you-ate by me, no pressure. :)

My brother, Paul: I love praying with you. Your passion for Jesus Christ is one thing I really admire. I'm so happy you have beat the odds!! You encourage me.

My tribe-sisters and longtime friends: Thank you for letting me be my quirky, witty, bust -out- in- random- dance- with -song self, all while being a true supernova. I love you all! (special thanks to Taneisha Smith :)

My sister-moms, Toya and Dionne: Thank you for believing in me and supporting me in every way possible. Thank you for feeding me LOL, I mean that. You know I do. I love you both, and any suitor wanting to marry you needs to know that I come with the package. It is written. *paints nails confidently*

My beautiful, gifted, FAVORED by God, sweet, sister Abriel. I stepped into a deeper place of intimacy with God because of you. GodTV. Kat Kerr. IHOP. All of our worship parties and mission possible prayer renegades. Please, do not ever let anyone, including yourself, kill that child like faith; it keeps God's fire inside of you lit. I wouldn't be here without you. I love you sister!!! (Aaron and J'oel, I love you, make Ma proud!)

Mommy: I miss you Mother. However, I'm glad you are enjoying Heaven! I'm forever committed to honoring your legacy. Keep praying for me up there. I love you.

Farah: Thank you for giving me space to be myself and enjoy my time with Heavenly Father. We are sisters, and all that you have done for me, I pray for God to bless you one thousand times more. I ate some of your popcorn earlier by the way, judge me later.

Jazmyn: I think you may be one of my first 'prayer disciples.' LOL. I had no idea!!! 'Alright Jazmyn, pray!!' All those prayers are in manifestation. So dope!! Watching you flourish in Christ is so beautiful!! I am here to always remind you of microwaved grilled cheese sandwiches and don't you ever let me forget that -12 degree late night. We're HERE now, let's enjoy this milk and honey!

To Ava: Thank you for pushing me to do this book!!! Well, pushing Mom too! :) You believed in this baby so much!! I remember you prophesying over me the magnitude of what writing this book means for the world, and the harvest attached to my obedience. I just had a sincere desire to send people prayers, one-on-one. *Shiena shrug* You saw the layers and pulled them back for me to see greater. You and mom are such a class act. Thank you!

To my editor, 'mom,' and woman I wish I was, if I lived in the 70's: Jean Dancy. This book would not be an excellent piece of showmanship without your ink on it. You made some pitty pats on my phone become official. Your input from start to finish has made the difference. I absolutely am overflowing with gratitude and humility that you agreed to be apart of this. You! Jean Dancy! *faints, then looks up with starry eyes and a whisper* You're amazing, thank you.

To the king and prophet who continues to wow me: You know God's voice, obey His voice, and believe in prayer. Thank you for being committed to your spiritual growth. It has changed my life. Your integrity, drive, faith and consistency to create and inspire everyday, motivated me to finish this endeavor. I have the honor of calling you friend...and I'm so HAPPY GLAD about it! Continue to Honor God in all that you do, from the inside out. Cheers to dominating!

Thank you to every person who trusted my spiritual integrity and allowed me to pray for them. It is humbling. You inspired this book!

I realize that I might have forgotten someone. This is similar to an artist winning their first award, and they go over the allotted 'thank you' time, but still name new people on the second win. Please forgive me! There will be other books, and I will most graciously acknowledge you. Continue to love me because I absolutely love you :) Oh! Cynthia Driver!! I'm manifesting :) Thank you for pushing me to manifest for myself!!!!! (See, they've cued the walk off music and I'm still talking. They're muting the microphone at this point. Gotta go....*lip miming now*

I

HEALING

God spoke the words "Be healed," and we were healed,
delivered from death's door!
Psalm 120:20 (TPT)

1

WHEN SOMEONE YOU LOVE HAS HURT YOU

Father, thank You that even though I am hurting, this isn't the end of my story. Thank You for balancing my emotions as my healing manifests. Thank You for freedom to cry as needed and thank You for replacing every feeling of pain with Your joy. I receive peace that passes all understanding through this process, because I don't always understand, but I still trust You.

Thank You for beautifying these ashes and giving me wisdom, so my emotions do not dictate my decisions. I surrender to Your love walk. Send me angels to show me the path of unconditional love. Close my ears from words tainted with bitter souls and contentment, help me to only heed to Your voice and counsel. In the name of Jesus Christ, Amen.

2

SCRIPTURES

Then God's wonderful peace that transcends human understanding, will make the answers known to you through Jesus Christ.
  Philippians 4:7 (TPT)

And I will give them singleness of heart and put a new spirit within them. I will take away their stony, stubborn heart and give them a tender, responsive heart.
  Ezekiel 11:19 (NLT)

God, I invite your searching gaze into my heart. Examine me through and through; find out everything that may be hidden within me. Put me to the test and sift through all my anxious cares. See if there is any path of pain I'm walking on, and lead me back to your glorious, everlasting ways—the path that brings me back to you.
  Psalm 139:23,24 (TPT)

3

OVERCOMING DEPRESSION

Abba Father, thank You that I can give everything to You. I give You this heaviness of depression in exchange for endless gratitude and joy. Thank You that my mourning is turning into dancing and I now have the desire to move around until I feel the change. Thank You that my perspective has changed to see things from heaven's point of view. I am a victor of my circumstance! I am loved by You and Your love overflows in every area of my life.

I bind the spirit of depression and its cohorts: insecurity, bitterness, negativity, trauma, cynicism, lethargy, uncleanliness and poverty. I choose as an act of my will to loose depression from my soul, now! I bind my soul to unconditional love in the name of Jesus; abundant life, joy prosperity, and peace. I breathe in peace, clarity and truth. I exhale old patterns keeping me bound.

Thank You Jesus that now I am receiving my freedom and I boldly walk in it, facing towards my future. It is done, in the name of Jesus Christ, amen.

Special note: There are many people silently suffering with depression and everyone's experience with being free is unique. Consider the options of speaking to a licensed counselor or a therapist to aide in your healing process. I also highly recommend SOZO, which is an in depth healing session.

4

SCRIPTURES

So keep your thoughts continually fixed on all that is authentic and real, honorable and admirable, beautiful and respectful, pure and holy, merciful and kind. And fasten your thoughts on every glorious work of God, praising him always.
Philippians 4:8 (TPT)

So now I live with the confidence that there is nothing in the universe with the power to separate us from God's love. I'm convinced that his love will triumph over death, life's troubles, fallen angels, or dark rulers in the heavens. There is nothing in our present or future circumstances that can weaken his love. There is no power above us or beneath us—no power that could ever be found in the universe that can distance us from God's passionate love, which is lavished upon us through our Lord Jesus, the Anointed One!
Romans 8:38-39 (TPT)

Yet when holy lovers of God cry out to him with all their hearts, the Lord will hear them and come to rescue them from all their

troubles.
  Psalm 34:17 (TPT)

5

GENERAL PHYSICAL HEALING

Heavenly Father, thank You for being Jehovah Rapha and healing my body of all imperfections and infirmities. Every symptom, diagnosis, ache, strain and discomfort coming against my health is dismantled by the Blood of Jesus Christ. Every ailment go to a dry place, now, and do not come back!

Body, I remind you that the Blood of Jesus Christ still works and you will come into agreement with this covenant, now. Body, line up with the promises of God for my life. Body, I remind you that my Abba Father loves me and YOU will surrender to His love, now.

I am healed and I see the manifestation immediately. In the name of Jesus, Christ, amen!

Special note: Take communion to honor the healing covenant in the Blood of Jesus Christ. Take it as often as you need to, just like you would take medicine. You can even intentionally take it with your medicine, by faith, believing for total healing. Jesus is a healing balm and His Blood is the perfect remedy for any sickness!

6

SCRIPTURES

I will give you back your health
  and heal your wounds." says the Lord
  Jeremiah 30:17 (NLT)

With my whole heart, with my whole life,
  and with my innermost being,
  I bow in wonder and love before you, the holy God!
  Yahweh, you are my soul's celebration.
  How could I ever forget the miracles of kindness
  you've done for me?
  You kissed my heart with forgiveness, in spite of all I've done.
  You've healed me inside and out from every disease.
  You've rescued me from hell and saved my life.
  You've crowned me with love and mercy.
  You satisfy my every desire with good things.
  You've supercharged my life so that I soar again
  like a flying eagle in the sky!
  Psalm 103 (TPT)

7

DIGESTIVE SYSTEM

Father, Jehovah Rapha, thank You for the authority to decree healing here on Earth. I send a word of settlement over bowels, intestines and stomachs. Ministering angels release anointings of healing and restoration over the human body. Holy Spirit reveal any spiritual imbalance that may be causing physical imbalance. I decree complete hydration, and an unusual craving for water. I decree diets are regulated with proper nutrients and protein. I thank You that all is well now. Thank You Jesus that Your blood was shed for this matter. Show Your glory now. In the name of Jesus Christ, Amen.

8

SCRIPTURES

Worship the Lord your God, and his blessing will be on your food and water. I will take away sickness from among you
   Exodus 23:25 (NIV)

With my whole heart, with my whole life,
   and with my innermost being,
   I bow in wonder and love before you, the holy God!
   Yahweh, you are my soul's celebration.
   How could I ever forget the miracles of kindness
   you've done for me?
   You kissed my heart with forgiveness, in spite of all I've done.
   You've healed me inside and out from every disease.
   You've rescued me from hell and saved my life.
   You've crowned me with love and mercy.
   You satisfy my every desire with good things.
   You've supercharged my life so that I soar again
   like a flying eagle in the sky!
   Psalm 103:1-5 (TPT)

9

BODY, SOUL & SPIRIT

Heavenly Father, thank You that we are drenched in the blood of Jesus Christ. It is our healing balm and we receive healing in our bodies, our souls and our spirits. We expect manifestation now as a testament of Your love for us. Thank You that tumors are disappearing and falling off. Thank You for new limbs growing, new blood vessels, new organs, new MINDSETS. Yes, thank You that pain is ceasing, even in our souls. Some of us have been sick in our souls because of hurt, betrayal and pain caused by those we trusted, but thank You for healing us.

Thank You for giving us freedom to abandon the strongholds of the enemy that made our spirit weary. We receive You in our spirit man. Whatever alarm our body is giving us to reveal a deeper issue, we open our ears to hear so we can walk in total healing. We release angels to excel in strength to hospital rooms, work desks, bedrooms and motor vehicles. Ministering angels you are released to perform the word of restoration and newness.

We shout wholeness to the broken and proclaim their healing can not be stolen. May their faith rise up to do what they could not do in their brokenness, as a sign to themselves that the healing virtue of Jesus has manifested. In the name of Jesus Christ, Amen.

10

SCRIPTURES

Beloved, I pray that in every way you may succeed and prosper and be in good health [physically], just as [I know] your soul prospers [spiritually].
   3 John 1:2 (AMP)

Now, may the God of peace and harmony set you apart, making you completely holy. And may your entire being—spirit, soul, and body—be kept completely flawless in the appearing of our Lord Jesus, the Anointed One. The one who calls you by name is trustworthy and will thoroughly complete his work in you.
   1 Thessalonians 5:23,24 (TPT)

II

TRAVEL

For it is written and forever remains written,

'He will command His angels concerning You to guard and protect You,'
Luke 4:10 (AMP)

11

DIVINE INTERFERENCE WITH TRAVEL

Father, I release angels assigned to (insert name). Let them detour and halt all trips local, national and international that are not in Your will. Your will be done, and nothing less. Quicken their spirit with unrest concerning places their feet are not graced to tread and let an overwhelming desire to be home consume their heart now, according to Your schedule for them. Disrupt communications for non ordained travel. Go angels now! I decree it done, in the name of Jesus Christ, Amen!

12

SCRIPTURES

When we live our lives within the shadow of God Most High,
   our secret hiding place, we will always be shielded from harm.
   How then could evil prevail against us or disease infect us?
   God sends angels with special orders to protect you wherever you go,
      defending you from all harm.
   If you walk into a trap, they'll be there for you
      and keep you from stumbling.
   You'll even walk unharmed among the fiercest powers of darkness,[h]
      trampling every one of them beneath your feet!
   For here is what the Lord has spoken to me:
   "Because you have delighted in me as my great lover,
      I will greatly protect you.
   I will set you in a high place, safe and secure before my face.
   I will answer your cry for help every time you pray,
      and you will find and feel my presence
      even in your time of pressure and trouble.
   I will be your glorious hero and give you a feast.

You will be satisfied with a full life and with all that I do for you.

For you will enjoy the fullness of my salvation!

Psalm 91:11-16 (TPT)

III

FINANCES

I am convinced that my God will fully satisfy every need you have, for I have seen the abundant riches of glory revealed to me through the Anointed One, Jesus Christ!

Philippians 4:19 (TPT)

13

FINANCIAL RELEASE

Heavenly Father, You said lack is not in Your will for me. I give You my concerns indefinitely. Thank You for keeping Your Word. I believe that You take great pleasure in me being well taken care of. I'm grateful for Your creative provision. My spirit is open to You and my hands are open to receive.

I remind You of my tithe and the promise You made to pour out a blessing, where I don't have enough room to receive it all. I release the angels of finance and provision, to bring me resources from the North, South, East, and West, now! I release angels to drop finances into my bank accounts, and may they multiply sevenfold. In the name of Jesus Christ, Amen.

14

SCRIPTURES

Make God the utmost delight and pleasure of your life, and he will provide for you what you desire the most.
  Psalm 37:4 (TPT)

Bring all the tithes into the storehouse so there will be enough food in my Temple. If you do," says the Lord of Heaven's Armies, "I will open the windows of heaven for you. I will pour out a blessing so great you won't have enough room to take it in! Try it! Put me to the test!
  Malachi 3:10 (NLT)

IV

DESTINY & PURPOSE

So we are convinced that every detail of our lives is continually woven together to fit into God's perfect plan of bringing good into our lives, for we are his lovers who have been called to fulfill his designed purpose.
Romans 8:28 (TPT)

15

KEEPING THE EGO SURRENDERED

Father God, thank You for the living example of Jesus Christ, to show us how to live everyday with a surrendered ego. When we experience the dichotomy of wanting to give up and wanting to persevere, thank You that Your faithfulness is great and trustworthy. You continue to encourage our spirits despite what is happening around us. We lean into that encouragement, we dive into grace right now.

The call to carry a cross is not easy but we understand the beauty of sacrifice, and we receive beauty for our ashes. What we have yet to understand, we receive peace. We receive the fruit of the spirit that is only harvested through this process of our ego dying. Yes, selfishness dying, so the selflessness of Your Love can truly live and flow in us. Greater is Your mercy for us, the new mercies that carry us every morning and every night.

Thank You for the opportunity to be chosen to carry out Your legacy. We love being here with You. Even when we cannot feel You, thank You for the knowing in our spirits that You are with us and You care. Thank You for the knowing that we are champions when we feel false defeat. Thank You that dying is really living. In the name of Jesus Christ, Amen.

16

SCRIPTURES

To truly know him meant letting go of everything from my past and throwing all my boasting on the garbage heap. It's all like a pile of manure to me now, so that I may be enriched in the reality of knowing Jesus Christ and embrace him as Lord in all of his greatness.
 Philippians 3:8 (TPT)

Jesus said to all of his followers, "If you truly desire to be my disciple, you must disown your life completely, embrace my 'cross' as your own, and surrender to my ways. For if you choose self-sacrifice, giving up your lives for my glory, you will embark on a discovery of more and more of true life. But if you choose to keep your lives for yourselves, you will lose what you try to keep.
 Luke 9:23,24 (TPT)

The faithful love of the Lord never ends! His mercies never cease.
 Lamentations 3:22,23 (NLT)

17

TRUSTING GOD IN SILENT MOMENTS

Father…thank You. Even though I get overwhelmed with the 'how' and 'why' sometimes, please help me so these moments do not overshadow my 'thank You.' Let Your river flowing of peace guide me in the silent moments of Your leadership. I receive that You just want me to trust You, without questions rooted in fear. I know that in You, fear doesn't exist because You are LOVE and You love me "good". Help me to love myself "good", unconditionally, without condemnation. I don't want condemnation, I want You and all that You said I am. Beauty. Royalty. Love. Thank You again. In the name of Jesus Christ, Amen.

18

SCRIPTURES

Now may God, the inspiration and fountain of hope, fill you to overflowing with uncontainable joy and perfect peace as you trust in him. And may the power of the Holy Spirit continually surround your life with his super-abundance until you radiate with hope!

Romans 15:13 (TPT)

It is the same with my word. I send it out, and it always produces fruit. It will accomplish all I want it to, and it will prosper everywhere I send it.

Isaiah 55:11 (NLT)

19

REMEMBERING YOUR PURPOSE AND DESTINY

Father, remind me of every promise You've given me, especially in the midst of adversity. Give me a divine recollection of my specific purpose in this earth, and who You called me to be before the world began. Also bring to my remembrance instructions to complete Heavenly assignments, and directives regarding those I am to bless. Thank You for keeping my name and face on the hearts of others that You've spoken to about me, until they carry out Your plans. Draw us with Your love and kindness to do Your will. May all distractions and fear cease. Angels of Divine Memory minister to us accordingly, so we can ultimately make God's name known in this world. In the name of Jesus Christ I decree it so, amen.

20

SCRIPTURES

So above all, constantly chase after the realm of God's kingdom[a] and the righteousness that proceeds from him. Then all these less important things will be given to you abundantly.

Matthew 6:33 (TPT)

Praise the Lord who has given rest to his people Israel, just as he promised. Not one word has failed of all the wonderful promises he gave through his servant Moses.

1 Kings 8:56 (NLT)

And I have filled him with the Spirit of God, with ability and intelligence, with knowledge and all craftsmanship, to devise artistic designs, to work in gold, silver, and bronze, in cutting stones for setting, and in carving wood, to work in every craft.

Exodus 31:3-5 (ESV)

21

MANIFESTING DREAMS

Heavenly Father, You're always right here waiting for me. I appreciate that about You. You said You are backing me up with my dreams; I'm so honored, excited and nervous all at the same time. You've showed me some huge dreams! Gave me some huge desires! However, thank You that the time is NOW and the process is over, it was yesterday. And I'm here in THIS moment, fully aware, present...so I know it's here. The moment I've been waiting for all my life. You've launched me into the deep, and I'm committed to trusting You and following Your Grace. It's never failed me yet. I receive Your love! In the name of Jesus Christ, Amen.

22

SCRIPTURES

O Lord our God, let your sweet beauty rest upon us
 and give us favor.
 Come work with us, and then our works will endure,
 and give us success in all we do.
 Psalm 90:17 (TPT)

23

PERSEVERE THROUGH THE PROCESS

Father thank You for the ability to see past our circumstances into the truth of our destiny.

Thank You for dreams that remind us of the finished works, that remind us of our success in Your love. Keep us grounded in that truth, give us the words to say to stomp out the lies of 'life happening.'

You have ordered our steps in Your perfect will, help us to choose that path over other roads led by fear, doubt and settlement. We were born to conquer and be great, and we believe it. Help us to continue to believe when reason and logic tempt us to sway. Give us hopeful affirmations filled with Your confirming love and compassion.

Thank You that throughout the journey of us being processed for our purpose, we are steadfast like a tree rooted by living waters. You quench our thirst with Your love; Your well of love that never runs dry! So we take a drink even now and are fulfilled in Your presence. We seek Your presence now, like never before. Welcome Holy Spirit into our thinking, into our emotions, into our will. In the name of Jesus Christ, Amen.

24

SCRIPTURES

They are like trees planted along a riverbank,
 with roots that reach deep into the water.
 Such trees are not bothered by the heat
 or worried by long months of drought.
 Their leaves stay green,
 and they never stop producing fruit.
 Jeremiah 17:8 (NLT)

The steps of the God-pursuing ones
 follow firmly in the footsteps of the Lord,
 and God delights in every step they take to follow him.
 Psalm 37:23 (TPT)

Their pleasure and passion is remaining true to the Word of "I Am,"
 meditating day and night in his true revelation of light.
 They will be standing firm like a flourishing tree
 planted by God's design,
 deeply rooted by the brooks of bliss,

bearing fruit in every season of their lives.
They are never dry, never fainting,
ever blessed, ever prosperous.
Psalm 1:2-3 (TPT)

Jesus answered, "If you drink from Jacob's well you'll be thirsty again and again, but if anyone drinks the living water I give them, they will never thirst again and will be forever satisfied! For when you drink the water I give you it becomes a gushing fountain of the Holy Spirit, springing up and flooding you with endless life!"
John 4:13-14 (TPT)

25

KEEPING DREAMS AT THE FEET OF GOD

Father, I trust You with my life dreams. I know You placed these dreams within me, and I'm surrendering them back to You. I'm letting go, freeing up that space for more of You. Whatever part of the process where I've added or taken away from these dreams; erase it, make it brand new again. Revive me with a zeal to believe and trust like never before. You are the God of exceedingly and abundantly; exceed what I've known these dreams to be, and let Your abundance overflow.

Thank You that my life dreams cannot be stolen. Thank You my life dreams cannot be replaced with Satan's plans for me; because I am Yours. You protect what belongs to You, so I am safe. My destiny is safe, my purpose is safe, my legacy is safe... .my dream is secured. I give You permission to manifest the dreams You've given me. I give You permission to move by Your Spirit in my life, in a greater miracle than before. Your presence, Your supernatural flow is welcome! I'm putting my foot on the gas and my hands off the wheel! I trust You, and I'm moving forward with faith and patience! I decree and declare it so.

My God given dreams are a finished work. My God given dreams are realized for the world to see, and to KNOW that Your Glory is real. In the name of Jesus Christ, Amen.

26

SCRIPTURES

Trust in the Lord completely and do not rely on your own opinions. With all your heart rely on him to guide you, and he will lead you in every decision you make. Become intimate with him in whatever you do, and he will lead you wherever you go. Don't think for a moment that you know it all, for wisdom comes when you adore him with undivided devotion and avoid everything that's wrong.
Proverbs 3:5-7 (TPT)

Never doubt God's mighty power to work in you and accomplish all this. He will achieve infinitely more than your greatest request, your most unbelievable dream, and exceed your wildest imagination! He will outdo them all, for his miraculous power constantly energizes you.
Ephesians 3:20 (TPT)

Submit to God, and you will have peace;
    then things will go well for you...
    You will succeed in whatever you choose to do,

and light will shine on the road ahead of you.
Job 22:21,28 (NLT)

27

VICTORY

Thank you Father for your unfailing love, You have proven Yourself to be omnipotent over and again. Show Your face in a deeper way, thank You for an encounter with You that encourages us in the face of adversity. The enemy will not triumph because You favor us and we call forth Your will God, to manifest within our minds.

Transform our thinking, stretch us to believe past what we see, past the reasoning, because our minds cannot fathom the greatness of Your Love and the greatness of the cross. You have the last word, as always, and we will wave the victory banner stained by Your blood that was shed for us. The world will know You stand for us and our families. Never against us. In the name of Jesus Christ, amen.

28

SCRIPTURES

Create a new, clean heart within me. Fill me with pure thoughts and holy desires, ready to please you.
 Psalm 51:10 (TPT)

I run straight for the divine invitation of reaching the heavenly goal and gaining the victory-prize through the anointing of Jesus.
 Philippians 3:14 (TPT)

29

BEING PURIFIED FOR PURPOSE

Thank You Lord for purification. Thank You for renewing hearts and repairing the broken pieces that life causes at times. Greater still is Your grace; the ability to do what we cannot do on our own. I shout grace-grace over the lives and the purposes of Your children. Reveal the bigger picture, and although Your process of promotion into seasons of acceleration is not easy or easily understood,You see us fit to endure and You cheer for us.

Thank You for angels cheering us on to finish the race with integrity, peace and strength established in Your word; including the tailor made words spoken in our dreams, divine conversations and encounters. Only what we do for Christ will last.

So thank You that nothing can come up against the destinies of Your chosen ones and prosper. Warriors of wisdom and grace are awakening and I thank You for it! May we always be loyal to Your call. In the name of Jesus Christ, Amen.

30

SCRIPTURES

No, despite all these things, overwhelming victory is ours through Christ, who loved us
 Romans 8:37 (TPT)

You can do your best to prepare for the battle,
 but ultimate victory comes from the Lord God.
 Proverbs 21:31 (TPT)

But we thank God for giving us the victory as conquerors through our Lord Jesus, the Anointed One.
 1 Corinthians 15:57 (TPT)

31

SURRENDERING GOD'S PROMISE

Father, thank You for the promise You have made to me. I agree with it manifesting. However, I cannot do this. It is only by Your Spirit. So I relax. I'm exhaling, knowing You have this all figured out.

I patiently wait, with Your joy stirring my belief. My eyes are upon You Father, I look to You. You hold the world in Your hands and I just simply believe that includes all the plans You have for me. Release an expectation of goodness in my spirit, let it run over until I can only praise and worship You. I believe my worship for You is a weapon of mass destruction. So anything attempting to block me from Your presence is removed now, as I lift my praise and worship to You alone.

My adoration is for You, Father King! You are my song and You are my voice! Sing through me songs of victory and I'll rejoice, because I know all battles are won and what You promised is a done deal. Thank You for Angels, assigned to this promise, that are aligning paths and doorways to greet me. Thank You.

You have and always will be the Promise Keeper.
In the name of Jesus Christ, Amen.

32

SCRIPTURES

And yet, O Lord, you are our Father.
   We are the clay, and you are the potter.
   We all are formed by your hand.
   Isaiah 64:8 (NLT)

It is not by force nor by strength, but by my Spirit, says the Lord of Heaven's Armies.
   Zechariah 4:6 (AMP)

My old identity has been co-crucified with Messiah and no longer lives; for the nails of his cross crucified me with him. And now the essence of this new life is no longer mine, for the Anointed One lives his life through me—we live in union as one! My new life is empowered by the faith of the Son of God who loves me so much that he gave himself for me, and dispenses his life into mine!
   Galatians 2:20 (TPT)

Beloved friends, what should be our proper response to God's marvelous mercies? I encourage you to surrender yourselves to God to be his sacred, living sacrifices. And live in holiness, experiencing all that delights his heart. For this becomes your genuine expression of worship.

Romans 12:1 (TPT)

V

ENCOURAGEMENT

And everything I've taught you is so that the peace which is in me will be in you and will give you great confidence as you rest in me. For in this unbelieving world you will experience trouble and sorrows, but you must be courageous, for I have conquered the world!
John 16:33 (TPT)

33

WHEN YOU ARE WEARY

Father God, let ministering angels be released now to Your children that are restless, weary and hurting, because of circumstances they do not have answers for in this moment...the unknown part of our walk with You. Let ministering angels bring them peace, healing and a reassurance in their faith.

You've called them to a path less travelled when it comes to believing in You; strengthen them. Take their stress and replace it with a calm knowing that You will never fail, no matter how high the wave comes to consume them. Help them walk on water with You, no matter the outcome...because You are STILL a Father that loves with an unfailing love.

Send them hugs that will rest their mind. Stir up their spirits to worship You in spite of.

I stand on their behalf right now with a Thank YOU; let my worship be intercession for them. We need You right now in a very non religious way. Thank You for revealing Yourself new.

A love that fights for us when we are hurting and want to give up. Thank You for standing tall in the hearts of Your children! In the name of Jesus Christ, Amen.

34

SCRIPTURES

Above the furious flood, the Enthroned One reigns,
 the King-God rules with eternity at his side.
 This is the one who gives his strength and might to his people.
 This is the Lord giving us his kiss of peace
 Psalm 29:10,11 (TPT)

Then God's wonderful peace that transcends human understanding, will make the answers known to you through Jesus Christ.
 Philippians 4:7 (TPT)

You will keep in perfect peace
 all who trust in you,
 all whose thoughts are fixed on you!
 Isaiah 26:3 (NLT)

He gives power to the weak
 and strength to the powerless.
 Isaiah 40:29 (NLT)

As soon as I pray, you answer me;
   you encourage me by giving me strength.
   Psalm 138:3 (NLT)

35

GOD'S GLORY BE REVEALED

Loving Father, let Your glory be revealed through us. Your glory, manifested Word, let it be revealed now. We are ready to fulfill purpose, what You've called us to do before we were born. We look past reason and logic. We seek Your revelation for where to be, and who to be with at the appointed time. We are committed to not missing our moment with You. No delay, no confusion. We march forward with Your favor working for us.

We release Angels of Purpose and Angels of Destiny to work on our behalf until we have fulfilled Heaven's mandate for our lives. What's been held up by self condemnation, trauma, and the spirit of sabotage is released under the Fire of God. HalleluYah! You are worthy Almighty God, of all the glory coming forth out of our hearts. Your MANIFESTED WORD coming forth out of our hearts! Thank You for Your perfect will being done. In the name of Jesus Christ, Amen!

36

SCRIPTURES

Jesus looked at her and said, "Didn't I tell you that if you will believe in me, you will see God unveil his power?"
John 11:40 (TPT)

Yes, all things work for your enrichment so that more of God's marvelous grace will spread to more and more people, resulting in an even greater increase of praise] to God, bringing him even more glory!
2 Corinthians 4:15 (TPT)

And I pray that he would unveil within you the unlimited riches of his glory and favor until supernatural strength floods your innermost being with his divine might and explosive power.
Ephesians 3:16 (TPT)

The Son is the dazzling radiance of God's splendor, the exact expression of God's true nature—his mirror image! He holds the universe together and expands it by the mighty power of his spoken word

SCRIPTURES

Hebrews 1:3 (TPT)

VI

ENDURANCE

*You need the strength of endurance to reveal the
poetry of God's will and then you receive the promise
in full*
Hebrews 10:36 (TPT)

37

TO ENDURE GROWING PAINS

Father, thank You for Your grace to endure this process. Help me Holy Spirit, help me Jesus. Give me a song to sing to stir my joy while You refine me into pure gold. Your love makes it worth it all. Open my eyes to Your love. Let me see myself in You more and more when I look in the mirror. Holy Spirit remove the desire for quick gratification or the temptation to settle because of fear and impatience. Noah stood believing You for 150 years! I am desiring such bravery that no matter what, I will not betray Your faithful love toward me. Thank You. In the name of Jesus Christ, Amen.

38

SCRIPTURES

But keep your hope to the end and you will experience life and deliverance.
 Matthew 24:13 (TPT)

And we pray that you would be energized with all his explosive power from the realm of his magnificent glory, filling you with great hope.
 Colossians 1:11 (TPT)

39

ENDURING DESPITE EMOTIONS

Heavenly Father, Your children are prepared to wait. Holy Spirit, will You help us with our emotions? Emotions confuse our faith at times. Give us clarity to believe fearlessly, like You said we have the power to do. Moreover, You've never lied to us. Holy Spirit help us to be integral in our relationship with You. We cannot wait, we cannot believe, we cannot trust in our own strength.

Thank You for rising up within our souls now and taking captive all the thoughts and feelings that would sabotage our identity. We are Your righteousness, help us to remember this truth. In the name of Jesus Christ, Amen.

40

SCRIPTURES

But those who trust in the Lord will find new strength.
　They will soar high on wings like eagles.
　They will run and not grow weary.
　They will walk and not faint.
　Isaiah 40:31 (NLT)

This is why the Scriptures say:
　Things never discovered or heard of before,
　things beyond our ability to imagine—
　these are the many things God has in store
　for all his lovers.

But God now unveils these profound realities to us by the Spirit. Yes, he has revealed to us his inmost heart and deepest mysteries through the Holy Spirit, who constantly explores all things.
　1 Corinthians 2:9 (TPT)

41

WHEN FEELING OVERWHELMED

Heavenly Father, I need You in this moment so I surrender and lean into Your love. I can not do what is before me, without Your help. Holy Spirit, guide me and show me which way is best. I decree Your great grace is flowing over me now! Thank You that I am walking in Your exceeding abundance! In the name of Jesus Christ, Amen.

42

SCRIPTURES

Now my beloved ones, I have saved these most important truths for last: Be supernaturally infused with strength through your life-union with the Lord Jesus. Stand victorious with the force of his explosive power flowing in and through you.
  Ephesians 6:10 (TPT)

But He answered me, "My grace is always more than enough for you, and My power finds its full expression through your weakness." So I will celebrate my weaknesses, for when I'm weak I sense more deeply the mighty power of Christ living in me.
  2 Corinthians 12:9 (TPT)

43

PEACE OF MIND

Heavenly Father, thank You for being the center of my focus. Silence all the crazy thoughts keeping me up at night. Thank You that my thoughts are submitted to the truth of Your love for me. My rest is in You, Jesus. Thank You for the ability to think on things that are peaceful, full of truth, full of goodness and full of Your unfailing love. Yes, fill my mind with what YOU think about me. I receive the steadfast mind of Jesus Christ, amen.

44

SCRIPTURES

Quiet your heart in his presence and pray;
   keep hope alive as you long for God to come through for you.
   And don't think for a moment that the wicked in their prosperity
   are better off than you.
   Psalm 37:7 (TPT)

VII

DIRECTION

*What joy overwhelms everyone who keeps the ways
of God, those who seek him as their heart's passion!
They'll never do what's wrong but will always choose
the paths of the Lord.*
PSALM 119:2,3 (TPT)

45

HELP WITH MAKING DECISIONS

Father show clearly what to say 'yes' to, and help me with my decision making. Holy Spirit, thank You for being my consultant. Give me a desire for Your wisdom and boldness. Prompt me to go into the direction that is good for me. Clearly and boldly shut the doors that You did not open. I decree a breaking of covenant with the spirit of settling and the spirit of confusion. I decree I am divinely aligned with Heaven to propel into the unknown of greatness. Let victory manifest in its fullness; never turning back to what is dried up and dead! In the name of Jesus Christ, Amen.

46

SCRIPTURES

Give me revelation about the meaning of your ways
   so I can enjoy the reward of following them fully.
Give me an understanding heart so that I can
passionately know and obey your truth.
Guide me into the paths that please you,
for I take delight in all that you say.
Cause my heart to bow before your words of wisdom
and not to the wealth of this world.
Help me turn my eyes away from illusions
so that I pursue only that which is true;
drench my soul with life as I walk in your paths.
Reassure me of your promises, for I am your beloved,
your servant who bows before you.
Defend me from the criticism I face
for keeping your beautiful words.
Psalm 119:33–39 (TPT)

47

FOR SURE DIRECTION

Abba Father, You alone illuminate the road before me. Let Your light shining within me be my compass. I only want Your path for me! Angels assigned to my destiny, go before me and clear the road of any distractions, traps or detours. In the name of Jesus Christ, Amen.

48

SCRIPTURES

Trust in the Lord completely,
   and do not rely on your own opinions.
   With all your heart rely on him to guide you,
   and he will lead you in every decision you make.
   Become intimate with him in whatever you do,
   and he will lead you wherever you go.
   Don't think for a moment that you know it all.
   Proverbs 3:5,6 (TPT)

VIII

RESOLVING CONFLICT

Brothers and sisters, don't ever grow weary in doing what is right.

2 Thessalonians 3:13 (TPT)

49

WHERE TENSION IS OR MAY BE PRESENT

Father of Peace and Humility, I surrender my ego to You. Holy Spirit rise up within me, so I'm not easily offended. Thank You that Your peace is my Umpire. In the name of Jesus Christ, Amen.

50

SCRIPTURES

Let your heart be always guided by the peace of the Anointed One, who called you to peace as part of his one body. And always be thankful.
Colossians 3:15 (TPT)

When the Lord is pleased with the decisions you've made, he activates grace to turn enemies into friends.
Proverbs 16:7 (TPT)

51

WHEN SURROUNDED BY ENEMIES

Lord of the Angel Armies, thank You for fighting for me. You love justice and I surrender my desire to seek revenge for a battle You've already won. Thank You for defending me and making my enemies my footstool. Holy Spirit uproot any bitterness or hate, help me to forgive, and allow You to take control. I believe that the table You have prepared in the presence of my enemies, is filled with goodness and grace and the banner of VICTORY. I am resting in YOU. In the name of Jesus Christ, Amen.

52

SCRIPTURES

Now I know, Lord, that you are for me,
 and I will never fear what man can do to me.
 For you stand beside me as my hero who rescues me.
 I've seen with my own eyes the defeat of my enemies.
 I've triumphed over them all!
 Lord, it is so much better to trust in you to save me
 than to put my confidence in someone else.
 Yes, it is so much better to trust in the Lord to save me
 than to put my confidence in celebrities.
 Once I was hemmed in and surrounded by those who don't love you.
 But by Yahweh's supernatural power I overcame them all!
 Psalm 118:6-10 (TPT)

53

WHEN ENEMIES ARE STUBBORN

Father I've prayed for these enemies to cease and desist, to go away into their own territory and they're choosing to stay. You are Lord of the Angel Armies, I ask You to smite my enemies out of Your jealous love for me. I give it to You, Jehovah Gibbor.

If You've ordained these individuals to salvation, who are being used to come against me, send laborers of Your Kingdom to minister to them. Otherwise, cast my enemies down sending them into the traps they set for me, boomerang their evil efforts towards me, back to them sevenfold. Grace me to dodge every fiery dart thrown my way.

I ask for justice and surrender my need for revenge. Let Your love reign justice! Let it be known, I serve thee Almighty God! Hosts of Heaven, you are released to fight for me! Thank You for eternal Victory! In the name of Jesus Christ, Amen.

54

SCRIPTURES

O Lord, fight for me! Harass the hecklers, accuse my accusers.
  Fight those who fight against me.
  Put on your armor, Lord; take up your shield and protect me.
  Rise up, mighty God! Grab your weapons of war
  and block the way of the wicked who come to fight me.
  Stand for me when they stand against me!
  Speak over my soul: "I am your strong Savior!"
  Humiliate those who seek my harm. Defeat them all!
  Frustrate their plans to defeat me and drive them back.
  Disgrace them all as they have devised their plans to disgrace
me.
  Blow them away like dust in the wind,
  with the Angel of Almighty God driving them back!
  Make the road in front of them nothing but slippery darkness,
  with the Angel of the Lord behind them, chasing them away!
  For though I did nothing wrong to them, they set a trap for
me,
  wanting me to fall and fail.
  Surprise them with your ambush, Lord,

and catch them in the very trap they set for me.
Let them be the ones to fail and fall into destruction!
Then my fears will dissolve into limitless joy;
my whole being will overflow with gladness
because of your mighty deliverance.
Everything inside of me will shout it out:
"There's no one like you, Lord!"
For look at how you protect the weak and helpless
from the strong and heartless who oppress them.
Psalm 35:1-10 (TPT)

55

WHEN HOLDING ONTO OFFENSE

Father God, help us to release offenses so they don't become escalated negative energy. We don't want to become the very thing You called us to stand against.

So we give thanks that Your joy is our strength. We give You permission to wreck us with Your joy and compassion! Pour Yourself onto us and we give You all of us in return; the ugly stuff too...because You KNOW us, nothing is hidden. So here, have it ALL.

We believe Your love is constant and powerful enough to override the waves of our emotions. Thank You now! Thank You for accepting us for who we are, and making us better. Making us a tangible 'You" here on Earth. In the name of Jesus Christ, Amen.

56

SCRIPTURES

Beloved, don't be obsessed with taking revenge, but leave that to God's righteous justice. For the Scriptures say:

"If you don't take justice in your own hands,
 I will release justice for you," says the Lord.
 Romans 12:19 (TPT)

I—yes, I alone—will blot out your sins for my own sake
 and will never think of them again.
 Isaiah 43:25 (NLT)

However, I say to you, love your enemy, bless the one who curses you, do something wonderful for the one who hates you,[a] and respond to the very ones who persecute you by praying for them
 Matthew 5:44 (TPT)

57

FORGIVENESS

Abba Father, we lean into Your compassion in this moment. Help us to forgive, the way you forgave us at the Cross, through your beloved Son Jesus Christ. We break free, by grace, from ego entanglements that feed us lies about forgiving. If you can forgive, surely we have the ability to walk in forgiveness.

Thank You for a heart to forgive ourselves. Release self compassion within us, no more self condemnation. We are free in Christ to forgive others, to forgive ourselves. There are no mistakes, no person, no thoughts of failure or low self esteem that will keep us from the freedom You have given us. We walk in the truth of forgiveness now, we walk in humility now. In the name of Jesus Christ, Amen.

58

SCRIPTURES

A wise person demonstrates patience,
  for mercy means holding your tongue.
  When you are insulted,
  be quick to forgive and forget it,
  for you are virtuous when you overlook an offense.
  Proverbs 19:11 (TPT)

Be imitators of God in everything you do, for then you will represent your Father as his beloved sons and daughters. 2 And continue to walk surrendered to the extravagant love of Christ, for he surrendered his life as a sacrifice for us. His great love for us was pleasing to God, like an aroma of adoration—a sweet healing fragrance
  Ephesians 5:1-2 (TPT)

Now, this is the goal: to live in harmony with one another and demonstrate affectionate love, sympathy, and kindness toward other believers. Let humility describe who you are as you dearly love one another. Never retaliate when someone treats you wrongly, nor insult those who insult you, but instead, respond by speaking a blessing over them—because a blessing is what God promised to give you. For the Scriptures tell us:

Whoever wants to embrace true life and find beauty in each day must stop speaking evil, hurtful words and never deceive in what they say. Always turn from what is wrong and cultivate what is good; eagerly pursue peace in every relationship, making it your prize. For the eyes of the Lord Yahweh rest upon the godly, and his heart responds to their prayers. But he turns his back on those who practice evil.
  1 Peter 3:8-10 (TPT)

59

WHEN FACING TEMPTATION

Faithful Constant One, thank You for giving us the supernatural strength to flee from temptation. Whether it be sex addictions, greed, dishonesty...whatever the vice, I know Your love is consistent to lead us to a life of victory that You promised us. We don't want to live under the weight of sin. You said Your grace is sufficient. Help us Jesus to conceive how great Your love is and that every temptation was conquered at the cross.

Renew our minds to be strengthened in Your Word of truth, so that we become free from walking a life in error. Holy Spirit shake us from the bondage of deception; destroy the chains now. Enlighten our eyes to have the perception of Your philosophy, not the ideals of the world, because the world doesn't love us.

The world seeks to be masters of our souls and destroy our spirits. Focus our lens to see CLEARLY, pass the smoke and mirrors that lust creates. We surrender the cravings of our flesh, because our flesh will never be satisfied. Only You can satisfy us. Everything, and everyone that comes from You builds us up, pushes us towards Your love.

Therefore remove anything and anyone, coming against our communion with you. Reveal every hidden plot and betrayal. We receive Your grace to obey Your instructions, and to hear YOUR voice.

Show us ourselves; where You desire to heal us. We trust You to walk us through the process. We trade in shame for Your unconditional love. Thank You for the resurrection of Jesus Christ at the Cross. This act of love for us was not in vain. Thank You for helping us to live a life that displays Your victory. In the name of Jesus Christ, Amen.

60

SCRIPTURES

He suffered and endured every test and temptation, so that he can help us every time we pass through the ordeals of life.
Hebrews 2:18 (TPT)

You need the strength of endurance to reveal the poetry of God's will and then you receive the promise in full.
Hebrews 10:36 (TPT)

61

JEALOUSY

Father bless (insert name of person/people you are jealous of) with far more than their heart desires. Accelerate them into their destiny, heal any open wounds with Your love. Help me trust You more, and confidently know You have no respect of persons. There is greatness for me too. Help me to receive my greatness and not compare myself to others. Thank You for Your perception of me; open my eyes to see myself like You do, then live like I believe it. In the name of Jesus Christ, Amen.

Special note: Jealousy is sneaky and will linger in the hidden parts of the soul. Pray these types of prayer with a firm belief, until you no longer feel the insecurity and jealousy towards that person when you think of them. Jealousy can have a very powerful effect on your thoughts and actions, but it is even more powerful to be free from jealousy! It has nothing to do with the person, yet everything to do with trusting God's love for YOU. God loves you forever!

62

SCRIPTURES

But if there is bitter jealousy or competition hiding in your heart, then don't deny it and try to compensate for it by boasting and being phony. For that has nothing to do with God's heavenly wisdom but can best be described as the wisdom of this world, both selfish and devilish. So wherever jealousy and selfishness are uncovered, you will also find many troubles and every kind of meanness.
   James 3:14-16 (TPT)

Let the dawning day bring me revelation
   of your tender, unfailing love.
   Give me light for my path and teach me, for I trust in you.
   Psalm 143:8 (TPT)

63

FOR DECEPTION TO BE REVEALED

Father God, You never forsake us, show us the truth. Reveal Your love to us; that it endures and it is present in our lives, even now in this moment. Every snake disguised, we cut it off at its head and everyone will know that our name is victory. There is no pit too deep that Your Love, Jesus, can't reach in and pull us out. So thank You for rescuing us from every deception of defeat. Reveal to us strategies for living a life of greatness. Reveal the keys to unlock our wealthy place, where joy is our portion. We are not deceived by mediocrity. Depression has no power over our minds.

We decree a paradigm shift to a mindset of truth, is our miracle today. We decree that You have rewritten our history and the places where failures deceived us, we are now victorious. Thank You that grace abounds in our destinies. In the name of Jesus Christ, Amen.

64

SCRIPTURES

He reveals deep and mysterious things
   and knows what lies hidden in darkness,
   though he is surrounded by light.
   Daniel 2:22 (NLT)

Ask me and I will tell you remarkable secrets you do not know about things to come.
   Jeremiah 33:3 (NLT)

IX

FAMILY

Love is large and incredibly patient. Love is gentle and consistently kind to all. It refuses to be jealous when blessing comes to someone else. Love does not brag about one's achievements nor inflate its own importance. Love does not traffic in shame and disrespect, nor selfishly seek its own honor. Love is not easily irritated or quick to take offense. Love joyfully celebrates honesty and finds no delight in what is wrong. Love is a safe place of shelter, for it never stops believing the best for others. Love never takes failure as defeat, for it never gives up.

1 Corinthians 13:4-7 (TPT)

65

PARENTING/LEGACY

Abba Father, thank You for the grace you have given to parents. May Your voice be heard through parents seeking to offer wise counsel to their children. May the parent experiencing conflict with their children avoid provoking them to rebellion. May these parents seek You, Holy Spirit, on the best strategy to raise their children, according to their individual life calling. Give them a plan for parenting that is rooted in Your word and remind them they are only stewards of whom they've dedicated to You. Let all selfish ambitions, whether by the parent or the child, become convicted by a true revelation of purpose.

Let divine destinies be revealed. Let true identities in Jesus Christ be embraced. Thank You that the Blood of Jesus Christ repels every plan to steal inheritances, create familial wedges and taint legacies.

Thank You that any time considered to be wasted or stolen, is redeemed by Your eternal grace. Thank you that any delays or detours are being used as a testimony of grace and mercy.

Thank You so much for showing Yourself strong and faithful. We will endure to the end. In the name of Jesus Christ, Amen.

66

SCRIPTURES

Look with wonder at the depth of the Father's marvelous love that he has lavished on us! He has called us and made us his very own beloved children.
1 John 3:1(a) (TPT)

This is my command—be strong and courageous! Do not be afraid or discouraged. For the Lord your God is with you wherever you go.
Joshua 1:9 (NLT)

67

HOPE FOR SINGLE PARENTS

Abba Father, for the Parent raising their child alone right now, I loose angels to minister peace and wisdom to them. Keep their heart soft with Your grace; heal any wounds with Your Agapé Love. Thank You for sending divine help and provision. Wherever the other parent is, even if deceased, I ask on this active parent's behalf that You fill the void in their children. I release divine connections for integral mentorship.

Heavenly Father keep the active parent anchored in hope, by Your love. Hope for a loving relationship that mirrors Your love. Hope that the best is yet to come, and their children are indeed called to be world changers. Hope to believe they are not truly alone, because You are with them and angels are assisting them with parenting.

You are a good, good Father, always and forever. I thank You that Your faithfulness towards us, keeps parents encouraged and steadfast to trust You always. May their lights SHINE for all to see through many generations. Let the raising of their children be seeds for an everlasting harvest of greatness, for several generations to come. In the name of Jesus Christ, Amen.

68

SCRIPTURES

So we are convinced that every detail of our lives is continually woven together to fit into God's perfect plan of bringing good into our lives, for we are his lovers who have been called to fulfill his designed purpose.
Romans 8:28 (TPT)

Children are God's love-gift; they are heaven's generous reward.
Children born to a young couple will one day rise to protect and provide for their parents.
Happy will be the couple who has many of them!
A household full of children will not bring shame on your name
but victory when you face your enemies,
for your offspring will have influence and honor to prevail on your behalf!
Psalm 127:3-5 (TPT)

Children, if you want to be wise, listen to your parents and do what they tell you, and the Lord will help you.

For the commandment, "Honor your father and your mother," was the first of the Ten Commandments with a promise attached: "You will prosper and live a long, full life if you honor your parents."

Fathers, don't exasperate your children, but raise them up with loving discipline and counsel that brings the revelation of our Lord.

Ephesians 6:1-5 (TPT)

69

WHEN FEELNG MISUNDERSTOOD

Heavenly Father, I ask that you go before me as my defender. Let the Blood of Jesus speak for me and cover my heart. Let angels be released on my behalf to minister to those in authority, about who I am and what I mean to You. I surrender the need to fight for myself because I believe and know that You have won for me. I walk in my victory now, with Your confidence living within me. Thank You for peace beyond what I understand, in the name of Jesus Christ, amen.

70

SCRIPTURES

The Lord himself will fight for you. Just stay calm.
   Exodus 14:14 (NLT)

Lord, you know everything there is to know about me.
   You perceive every movement of my heart and soul,
   and you understand my every thought before it even enters my mind.
   You are so intimately aware of me, Lord.
   You read my heart like an open book
   and you know all the words I'm about to speak
   before I even start a sentence!
   You know every step I will take before my journey even begins.
   Psalm 139:1-3, 6 (TPT)

71

FATHERS WHO ARE SEPARATED FROM THEIR CHILDREN

Heavenly Father, to the man who is longing to be a father to his children and is facing roadblocks from a bitter mother and her family: Show Yourself strong. Uncover all the lies told to keep him bound. I decree the system working for him and not against him. I decree a special favor with the judge; clear all smoke and mirrors.

Ministering angels, encourage him to keep pressing in integrity, to be bold and confident in his fatherhood. Cover the children/child. Give them insight into the truth of the matter; protect them from eternal bruises of feeling abandoned and unloved. That's a lie!

Moreover, whatever residue of the romantic or sexual relationship that has created bitterness, resentment, anger or vengeance in the heart of the mother, I decree a release now. A letting go, unravel their fists, change their posture to a stance of gratitude because children are a blessing and YOU, Almighty

God, do all things well. It IS well, in the name of Jesus Christ, amen.

72

SCRIPTURES

He heals the wounds of every shattered heart.
   He sets his stars in place, calling them all by their names.
   How great is our God!
   There's absolutely nothing his power cannot accomplish,
   and he has infinite understanding of everything.
   Psalm 147:3-5 (TPT)

Beloved, don't be obsessed with taking revenge, but leave that to God's righteous justice. For the Scriptures say:

"If you don't take justice in your own hands,
   I will release justice for you," says the Lord.
   Romans 12:19 (TPT)

The Lord loves seeing justice on the earth.
   Anywhere and everywhere you can find his faithful, unfailing love!
   Psalm 33:5 (TPT)

73

CONCERNING BARRENNESS

Everlasting Father, honor the desire of every woman longing to bring life through her womb. Bring forth Your promise with a bold ' Yes! Your HEAVENLY FATHER did this!'

I call forth life and declare barrenness is no more. I call forth creative miracles to manifest in the reproductive system, in both the man and woman. Every curse of infertility sent from darkness to abort royal legacies, I declare they are null and void. I speak blessings of plenty. I speak abundance in life giving. You are truly giving beauty for ashes. Let tears of joy flow in double portions for every moment of sorrow. In the name of Jesus Christ, Amen.

74

SCRIPTURES

Now faith brings our hopes into reality and becomes the foundation needed to acquire the things we long for. It is all the evidence required to prove what is still unseen.

Hebrews 11:1 (TPT)

There will be no miscarriages or infertility in your land, and I will give you long, full lives.

Exodus 23:26 (NLT)

Not one promise from God is empty of power, for nothing is impossible with God!"

Then Mary responded, saying, "This is amazing! I will be a mother for the Lord! As his servant, I accept whatever he has for me. May everything you have told me come to pass." And the angel left her.

Luke 1:37-38 (TPT)

75

FOR BARREN WOMEN TO PRAY OVER THEMSELVES

Heavenly Father, You are the giver of life and I thank you that my womb is in Your hand. Thank you for wisdom and discernment of Your timing. I break every agreement with the diagnosis of doctors that do line up with Your will for my life, and my family. I come into agreement with Heaven that I am a producer, a nurturer, and I am birthing Your legacy here on Earth.

Thank You for peace that passes what I understand. Thank You that our peace causes all anxiety, worry and shame to bow down.

Thank You for greater revelation of Your perfect love for me that casts out fear from the root. Thank You for giving me a song to sing that brings forth my promise children! In the name of Jesus Christ amen.

76

SCRIPTURES

Sing, barren woman, who has never had a baby.
   Fill the air with song, you who've never experienced childbirth!
   You're ending up with far more children
   than all those childbearing women." God says so!
   Isaiah 54:1-4 (MSG)

A thief has only one thing in mind—he wants to steal, slaughter,[a] and destroy. But I have come to give you everything in abundance, [b] more than you expect[c]—life in its fullness until you overflow!
   John 10:10 (TPT)

Now faith brings our hopes into reality and becomes the foundation needed to acquire the things we long for. It is all the evidence required to prove what is still unseen.
   Hebrews 11:1 (TPT)

Since we have this confidence, we can also have great boldness before him, for if we present any request agreeable to his will, he will hear us. And if we know that he hears us in whatever we ask, we also know that we have obtained the requests we ask of him.

1 John 5:14-15 (TPT)

77

PREGNANCY AND LABOR

God of joy and peace, I declare YOUR joy and peace over every pregnancy and labor. Father, You sent Jesus Christ to redeem us from the curse. I believe that the pain given for childbearing through Eve does not have to be our portion. I shout grace and more grace over labor and delivery. Let everyone experience the beauty of a God given miracle that we call childbirth. Relieve the pain. I command the atmosphere to be one of serenity.

Divinely connect doctors and nurses that are sensitive and well endowed with Godly wisdom. I decree and declare short deliveries and short recoveries. I bind every thought of depression and decree that postpartum does not bear any fruit. Your joy overflows.

Let the beauty of Your love embrace those mothers to see THEMSELVES as worthy and beautiful from the beginning of pregnancy to after their children are born.

Thank You that fathers will see these mothers as queens, full of honor and glory even the more after birthing their seed; building them up with words of appreciation, encouragement and gratitude. I decree teamwork and come against vainglory or division. Thank You for manifesting this; I believe all things are possible. In the name of Jesus Christ, Amen.

78

SCRIPTURES

You have shown me the way of life,
 and you will fill me with the joy of your presence.
 Acts 2:28 (NLT)

You are altogether beautiful, my darling,
 beautiful in every way.
 Song of Solomon 4:7 (NLT)

And we pray that you would be energized with all his explosive power from the realm of his magnificent glory, filling you with great hope.

Your hearts can soar with joyful gratitude when you think of how God made you worthy to receive the glorious inheritance freely given to us by living in the light.
 Colossians 1:11-12 (TPT)

This is my command—be strong and courageous! Do not be afraid or discouraged. For the Lord your God is with you wherever you go.

Joshua 1:9 (NLT)

And I find that the strength of Christ's explosive power infuses me to conquer every difficulty.
Philippians 4:13 (TPT)

X

RELATIONSHIPS & MARRIAGE

Above all, constantly echo God's intense love for one another, for love will be a canopy over a multitude of sins.

1 PETER 4:8 (TPT)

79

WHEN A LOVED ONE HAS TRANSITIONED

Father, thank You for doing ALL things well, You've welcomed Your child home and we yield to Your glory being revealed because of it. I thank You now for ministering Angels on assignment to comfort and encourage those who have been affected. I decree order and unity through this process and a peace to cover them.

Let Your love reign supreme and YOUR will be honored above all else. When we worship You, the enemy is silenced, so let all planning and preparation bring You glory, all egos be relinquished. Let Your Spirit of excellence be released. I declare a special blessing of rest and wonderful sleep over everyone affected by this transition. Thank You again for ordering the steps of Your children and telling Your child, 'Well done.' Thank You for showing Yourself to BE strength, when we are weak. In the name of Jesus Christ, Amen.

80

SCRIPTURES

I urge you, my brothers and sisters, for the sake of the name of our Lord Jesus Christ, to agree to live in unity with one another and put to rest any division that attempts to tear you apart. Be restored as one united body living in perfect harmony. Form a consistent choreography among yourselves, having a common perspective with shared values.

1 Corinthians 1:10 (TPT)

I leave the gift of peace with you—my peace. Not the kind of fragile peace given by the world, but my perfect peace. Don't yield to fear or be troubled in your hearts—instead, be courageous!

John 14:27 (TPT)

81

GETTING THROUGH GRIEF

Heavenly Father, thank You for being with me every step of the way as I adjust to (insert name of person who has passed away), no longer being here. I surrender the urge to be strong and receive Your grace to heal. Thank You for the capacity to grieve and the space to learn more about who I am in this process. I release all anger, worry, anxiety, depression and ask You, Holy Spirit, to comfort me. I receive gratitude. Remind me of moments that will stir joy inside of me and give me peace; especially when I do not understand the "why." Thank You for Your love that continues to surround me in new ways that I feel, see and share with others. In the name of Jesus Christ, Amen.

82

SCRIPTURES

The Lord is close to all whose hearts are crushed by pain,
   and he is always ready to restore the repentant one.
   Psalm 34:18 (TPT)

Don't be pulled in different directions or worried about a thing. Be saturated in prayer throughout each day, offering your faith-filled requests before God with overflowing gratitude. Tell him every detail of your life, then God's wonderful peace that transcends human understanding, will make the answers known to you through Jesus Christ. So keep your thoughts continually fixed on all that is authentic and real, honorable and admirable, beautiful and respectful, pure and holy, merciful and kind. And fasten your thoughts on every glorious work of God, praising him always.
   Philippians 4:6-8 (TPT)

I will never forget this awful time,
   as I grieve over my loss.
   Yet I still dare to hope

when I remember this:

The faithful love of the Lord never ends!
   His mercies never cease.
   Great is his faithfulness;
   his mercies begin afresh each morning.
   Lamentations 3:20-23 (NLT)

83

FREEDOM FROM TOXIC SOUL TIES

Heavenly Father, thank You for the grace and authority to break free from relationships that separate me from Your love. Thank You for revealing the truth that has been hidden by insecurities, rejection, abandonment, manipulation and seduction. I cut every toxic soul tie at the silver cord and the memory of it from my heart, mind, and GI tract. I will no longer experience anxiety or feel ill when I see them. I am consumed in everlasting joy and peace. I call back to me the pieces of my soul that was compromised. I receive wholeness in my soul.

Thank You for the strength to confront my wounds, so I can soar like an eagle and live in an atmosphere conducive to growing in Agape Love. Thank You that Your love rewrites the history in my heart. I decree and declare a revelation of my divine identity is propelling me into my God given purpose, and I now see life from an aerial view. I thank You that my today is GREATER than my yesterday, and all residue from these toxic soul ties are dissolved by Your love, NOW. In the name of Jesus Christ, amen.

84

SCRIPTURES

Yes, remember your Creator now while you are young, before the silver cord of life snaps and the golden bowl is broken. Don't wait until the water jar is smashed at the spring and the pulley is broken at the well.
Ecclesiastes 12:6 (NLT)

Let me be clear, the Anointed One has set us free—not partially, but completely and wonderfully free! We must always cherish this truth and stubbornly refuse to go back into the bondage of our past.
Galatians 5:1 (TPT)

Out of my deep anguish and pain I prayed,
   and God, you helped me as a father.
   You came to my rescue and broke open the way
   into a beautiful and broad place.
   Psalm 118:5 (TPT

85

TRUSTING COMPLETELY AND LOVING UNCONDITIONALLY

Abba Father, help me to trust You with giving You my heart; help me to be vulnerable. This is is the only way I will be able to love unconditionally and trust others. Help me Holy Spirit to discern who has the capacity to receive Love and give Love. Heal me from rejection so I can trust You completely and the people You send into my life. Show me how to get out of the way of this masterpiece You're making within.

Your heart is so resilient. Thank You for giving me Your heart in place of my battered one. Thank you for holding me in Your arms and giving me a space to heal without self righteous judgement. I love you and I receive Your love for me! In the name of Jesus Christ, Amen.

86

SCRIPTURES

And I will give you a new heart, and I will put a new spirit in you. I will take out your stony, stubborn heart and give you a tender, responsive heart.
   Ezekiel 36:26 (NLT)

And may the Lord increase your love until it overflows toward one another and for all people, just as our love overflows toward you.
   1 Thessalonians 3:12 (TPT)

87

GRACE TO LOVE UNCONDITIONALLY

Heavenly Father, there are some that You've graced to love people through the storm in their relationships. Make it clear the boundaries You've set for them. Make it clear HOW to love because some must love close up, and some must love far away; let their path of Love be defined.

Thank You that people are hearing Your clarion call to love unconditionally and are committed to the process of their "love perception" being renewed. Help us to love like You; not like the world. Selfless, everlasting and pure love is the love we give and receive. Let that be our life's testimony! In the name of Jesus Christ, amen and amen!

88

SCRIPTURES

Love is large and incredibly patient. Love is gentle and consistently kind to all. It refuses to be jealous when blessing comes to someone else. Love does not brag about one's achievements nor inflate its own importance. Love does not traffic in shame and disrespect, nor selfishly seek its own honor. Love is not easily irritated or quick to take offense. Love joyfully celebrates honesty and finds no delight in what is wrong. Love is a safe place of shelter, for it never stops believing the best for others. Love never takes failure as defeat, for it never gives up.

1 Corinthians 13:4-7 (TPT)

You are always and dearly loved by God! So robe yourself with virtues of God, since you have been divinely chosen to be holy. Be merciful as you endeavor to understand others, and be compassionate, showing kindness toward all. Be gentle and humble, unoffendable in your patience with others. Tolerate the weaknesses of those in the family of faith, forgiving one another in the same way you have been graciously forgiven by

Jesus Christ. If you find fault with someone, release this same gift of forgiveness to them. For love is supreme and must flow through each of these virtues. Love becomes the mark of true maturity.

Colossians 3:12-14 (TPT)

89

FOR A TROUBLED MARRIAGE

Heavenly Father, I surrender my covenant to You. I repent from any selfish ambitions. I thank You that my ego has no power in my decision making and decree selfless strategies are coming to me, that give You glory. Thank You for Godly wisdom and the sensitivity to hear Your voice. I partner with heaven and decree that I will not stay in this marriage for security, for the children, for reputation or for convenient sex. I will be in covenant because I've heard from You about my spouse and Your purpose for us.

I decree any illegal emotional ties are null and void. Thank You for Your grace rising within me to confront matters of the heart, with vulnerability and Agape Love. Thank You for the grace to forgive. Thank You for enlightening my eyes of understanding so I can see clearly Your plans for my life, and my covenant marriage. In the name of Jesus Christ, amen.

90

SCRIPTURES

So there you have it. What God has joined together, no one has the right to split apart.
  Mark 10:9 (TPT)

For love is supreme and must flow through each of these virtues. Love becomes the mark of true maturity.
  Colossians 3:14 (TPT)

With tender humility and quiet patience, always demonstrate gentleness and generous love toward one another, especially toward those who may try your patience. Be faithful to guard the sweet harmony of the Holy Spirit among you in the bonds of peace, being one body and one spirit, as you were all called into the same glorious hope of divine destiny.
  Ephesians 4:2-4 (TPT)

Finally, beloved friends, be cheerful! Repair whatever is broken among you, as your hearts are being knit together in perfect unity. Live continually in peace, and God, the source of love and peace, will mingle with you. Greet and embrace one another with the sacred kiss.

2 Corinthians 13:11-12 (TPT)

91

DIVINE MARRIAGES

Father God, thank You for divine marriages. I decree that we, Your children, are entering covenants graced in compassion, forgiveness and prosperity. I thank You that we are quick to seek Your thoughts about who we choose to love, over the opinions of people and even over our own wants. You know the intricate details of our being, You know what's best for us.

I decree and declare we are guided by Your endorsed choices, not decisions based on our emotions or the world's theology about relationships. Let us join with people who think like You and exude Your love for us. I call forth supernatural love in relationships that are slow to anger and quick to dwell in Your presence.

You are a God of covenant; remind us of the promises we have made to YOU. Surely it will lead us to the right people in our lives. Let us be examples to the world of what grace based families look like. Every lustful distraction, every gesture filled with pride, it has no power in our lives. We walk boldly with the love of Christ as our foundation. May we look to YOU for wisdom and guidance, closing our spirits off from bitter advice.

Let us not be open to average moral thinking or religious potholes. Let us stay clear from anything that will cloud our walk with You, on the journey of divine marriage. We receive Your vision so we can gratefully embrace our destiny mates. Thank You for the gift of marriage, the gift of family; we treasure it. In the name of Jesus Christ, amen.

92

SCRIPTURES

Go ahead and make all the plans you want,
   but it's the Lord who will ultimately direct your steps.
   We are all in love with our own opinions,
   convinced they're correct.
   But the Lord is in the midst of us,
   testing and probing our every motive.
   Before you do anything,
   put your trust totally in God and not in yourself.
   Then every plan you make will succeed.
   The Lord works everything together to accomplish his purpose.
   Proverbs 16:1-4a (TPT)

For I know the plans I have for you," says the Lord. "They are plans for good and not for disaster, to give you a future and a hope.
   Jeremiah 29:11(NLT)

And may the Lord our God show us his approval

and make our efforts successful.
Yes, make our efforts successful!
Psalm 90:17 (TPT)

XI

TALENTS/GIFTS/BUSINESS ENDEAVORS

So above all, constantly chase after the realm of God's kingdom[a] and the righteousness that proceeds from him. Then all these less important things will be given to you abundantly.
Matthew 6:33 (TPT)

93

CREATIVE POWER AND GIFTS

Heavenly Father, I ask that You open our minds and spirits to flow in Your creative power. I decree and declare freedom from agreements with creative ideas, that come from the Evil one in disguise. You are the True Creator and we trust You to give us ideas, inventions, songs, and artistic expressions that will bring us prosperity.

Thank You that we flow humbly in Your creativity with a surrender from pride, arrogance and ego. We agree that the glory does not belong to us, it is for Your glory alone. Thank You that we are Your vessels of creation and we do not make pacts with any other powers or gods. Thank you that our environments and the atmospheres that we place ourselves in, line up with Your Creative Holy Spirit. In the name of Jesus Christ, Amen.

94

SCRIPTURES

You will find true success when you find me,
 for I have insight into wise plans that are designed just for you.
 I hold in my hands living-understanding, courage, and strength.
 They're all ready and waiting for you.
 Proverbs 8:14 (TPT)

He was the one who prayed to the God of Israel, "Oh, that you would bless me and expand my territory! Please be with me in all that I do, and keep me from all trouble and pain!" And God granted him his request.
 1 Chronicles 4:10 (NLT)

95

FAVOR IN BUSINESS AND INFLUENCE IN CITY

Thank You Father for the unstoppable vision You've given us. I decree an activation of favor extended to us with our city. They will say 'yes,' when logic says 'no.' They will have to acknowledge that we belong to You. Increase our capacity of what we can see, so we will be steadfast in our belief. Let us complete every assignment we have been called to with an anointing of ease.

We believe and decree that everything needed to carry out our calling is looking for us. What a great manager You are! Continue to show us business savvy wisdom through our prayer time and team of support. We thank You for business contracts and deals that transition our realm of influence. We decree that our cities are now wells of selfless giving. We accept becoming beacons of light in our cities that exposes darkness hidden in high places. Every system in our reach will experience a righteous revolution. The Kingdom of God will be the normalcy in our city because, You have given us the authority to call

Heaven here in Earth. In the name of Jesus Christ, Amen.

96

SCRIPTURES

We have become his poetry, a re-created people that will fulfill the destiny he has given each of us, for we are joined to Jesus, the Anointed One. Even before we were born, God planned in advance our destiny and the good works we would do to fulfill it!
Ephesians 2:10 (TPT)

Be willing to be made low before the Lord and he will exalt you!
James 4:10 (TPT)

And we pray that you would be energized with all his explosive power from the realm of his magnificent glory, filling you with great hope
Colossians 1:11 (TPT)

97

FOR CREATIVES

Father I lift up to You, the creative community. Thank You that they are constantly seeking You for Your wisdom and are cloaked in humility. I declare wholeness over their souls, so they are not susceptible to ploys on any tethered emotions or wounds. Thank You that they are committed to being loyal to You; the giver of their gifts and talents. Thank You that they refuse to sell their anointing for quick fame, acceptance or spotlights.

Thank You for grace protecting them and the anointing on their lives. Let the gift of Godly discernment be their compass, when choosing opportunities and relationships. Let their eyes be open to SEE Truth, when smoke and mirrors are present.

Restore those who have become tainted from disappointments and trauma, to purity and childlike faith. Thank You that Your love has fought the battle and they are victorious from every trap set under the influence of 'Jezebel' and 'Delilah.' Thank You for their freedom from the chains of every sexual immoral encounter. No matter the seduction, the lust, the allusions, the betrayals....Your truth reigns and breathes life into their divine destinies.

I declare freedom from destructive habits and the spirit of addiction. I declare supernatural courage is rising up to confront any anxiety or fear. They will not bow to the God of this world. Your word will never pass away. So I rejoice now that every promise You've spoken over their lives has full fruition, in divine timing, for Your glory alone. In the name of Jesus Christ, Amen.

98

SCRIPTURES

Beloved friends, what should be our proper response to God's marvelous mercies? I encourage you to surrender yourselves to God to be his sacred, living sacrifices. And live in holiness, experiencing all that delights his heart. For this becomes your genuine expression of worship.

Stop imitating the ideals and opinions of the culture around you, but be inwardly transformed by the Holy Spirit through a total reformation of how you think. This will empower you to discern God's will as you live a beautiful life, satisfying and perfect in his eyes.
Romans 12:1-2 (TPT)

I pray that the Father of glory, the God of our Lord Jesus Christ, would impart to you the riches of the Spirit of wisdom and the Spirit of revelation to know him through your deepening intimacy with him.

I pray that the light of God will illuminate the eyes of your imagination, flooding you with light, until you experience the full revelation of the hope of his calling—that is, the wealth of God's glorious inheritances that he finds in us, his holy ones!

I pray that you will continually experience the immeasurable greatness of God's power made available to you through faith. Then your lives will be an advertisement of this immense power as it works through you! This is the mighty power.

Ephesians 1:17-19 (TPT)

99

PRAYER FOR THE PRESIDENT OF THE UNITED STATE/UNITED STATES

Heavenly Father, Your divine purpose prevail in the United States of America. May believer's rise above the emotional response from the chaos,and center themselves in a position of authority to decree divine destiny over families, cities, nations and countries around the world.

I decree President Trump's heart is postured in humility and wisdom. I decree President Trump and his administration are hearing the strategy of heaven with a conviction of passionate obedience. I decree the nation of the United States is marked with purity and righteousness. I decree the United States is aligning with God's decree over it.

In the name of Jesus Christ, amen.

100

SCRIPTURES

It's as easy for God to steer a king's heart for his purposes
as it is for him to direct the course of a stream.
Proverbs 21:1 (TPT)

Most of all, I'm writing to encourage you to pray with gratitude to God. Pray for all men with all forms of prayers and requests as you intercede with intense passion. And pray for every political leader and representative, so that we would be able to live tranquil, undisturbed lives, as we worship the awe-inspiring God with pure hearts.
1 Timothy 2:1-2 (TPT)

Then if my people who are called by my name will humble themselves and pray and seek my face and turn from their wicked ways, I will hear from heaven and will forgive their sins and restore their land.
2 Chronicles 7:14 (NLT)

XII

DECREE OVER YOURSELF

*You will also decree a thing, and it will be established
for you; And light will shine on your ways.*
Job 22:8 NASB
*What you decide on will be done, and light will shine
on your ways.*
Job 22:8 NIV

101

DAILY DECREE

Heavenly Father,

Thank You for the authority in Jesus Christ to a decree and establish a thing here on earth, as it is in heaven.

I decree that angels are excelling in strength now to align things in the spirit realm for earthly manifestation regarding my purpose and destiny.

I decree all hindrances and diabolical blockages are severed and removed, concerning my assignment for God's kingdom here in Earth.

I veto every diabolical sabotage concerning my destiny and purpose that carries over into three generations. I release divine strategies of wisdom, witty ideas and inventions that will accelerate my family's GOD ordained inheritance. We are legacy leavers, grounded in Agapé Love.

I decree a release to run through open doors and soar like eagles, concerning my divine mantle of authority, as Your Love Ambassador.

Father, I decree and declare that every possession You've given me steward over is looking for me. I call my land forth, modes of transportation, investments and multi million dollar deals that will release influence in the world system for Your kingdom system. I call forth every harvest promised and activated, through sowing and spiritual inheritance. I lack no good thing! I am not delayed or denied! I am accelerating!

I decree a release of Your Glory Father, in a deeper dimension; the weight of Your glory rests upon me. I receive You, Your love, Your vision and Your wisdom to walk in light and truth as Your child; as Your Messenger. It is so, I establish these words now, they can not be reversed and I will not take them back.

Angel of Promise excel in strength now, releasing manifesting miracles of Father's promises over my life. Wind of Change Angel go forth now on my behalf and bring my life into divine alignment. In the name of Jesus Christ I decree it so. I give You thanks, amen!!

XIII

WHAT I BELIEVE

102

STATEMENT OF FAITH

I believe the Bible is inspired and empowered by God. It is the highest authority, containing spiritual keys to operate as a citizen and ambassador of God's Kingdom.

I believe in one eternal God who exists as three separate persons; the Father, Holy Spirit and Son (Jesus Christ). I believe Satan exists, demons are real and use people to carry out plans for the Kingdom of Darkness in the Earth realm.

I believe Jesus Christ is the Son of God, born supernaturally of a virgin, lived a sinless life as He walked among men, demonstrated the authority and power of God in works and speech, died on the cross, resurrected supernaturally and is now seated at the right hand of God having accomplished all that is necessary for man's salvation.

I believe it is essential for man to repent of sin, meaning to change their mindset and turn away from it. I believe that by faith men can receive the finished work of Christ by confessing Him as Lord with his mouth, and believing it in his heart, resulting in a process of renewal by Holy Spirit.

I believe the Holy Spirit is continuing the work He started

at Pentecost, empowering believers to live a Godly life and advance the Kingdom of God. I believe in the many gifts of Holy Spirit (word of knowledge, gift of prophecy, different kind of tongues, the interpretation of tongues, word of wisdom, gift of faith, discerning of spirits). I believe in the baptism of Holy Spirit that releases a heavenly language of tongues to equip believers with supernatural power, that also edifies their spirit and gives an increased divine connection when conversing with God.

I believe in the return of Jesus Christ, and those who have believe in Him will experience a heavenly dwelling in an incorruptible body. I believe those who have rejected believing in Jesus Christ will join Satan and his Kingdom of Darkness in an eternal fire.

I believe the true Church is made up of born-again believers of Jesus Christ, regardless of denomination affiliations.

I believe all born-again believers have been commissioned to share the complete Gospel (His Grace) to all the world healing the sick, casting out demons and raising the dead.

I believe the gift of Grace is given to us by God because God desires us to have it, not because of anything we have done to earn it, and it is made available to those who receive it by faith.

103

TEACHERS I LOVE

Here are a few of my go-to's for spiritual food and as a complement to my personal studies:

Earlie James, Jr.

Dr. Cindy Trimm

Dr. Creflo Dollar

Tiphani Montgomery

Graham Cooke

Dr. Myles Munroe

104

PRAYER OF SALVATION

Father God, I believe that You sent Your only son Jesus Christ to die for all of my sins. Through His death I have been redeemed and forgiven from the eternal consequences of sin. Everything that I need and want to be a winner in life, was made available to me because of Jesus's death and resurrection. I receive Your love for me through this act, and I receive Your grace to be called Your child. Holy Spirit I welcome You to dwell within me, and navigate me through life to be an Ambassador for God's Kingdom. In the name of Jesus Christ, Amen.

If you prayed this with sincere belief, you have just received eternal salvation! What an awesome moment! I encourage you to connect with other believers for accountability and support as you begin the journey of walking out God's divine will for your life! This is just beginning!

Welcome to the Kingdom of God!

105

SCRIPTURES

For this is how much God loved the world—he gave his one and only, unique Son as a gift.So now everyone who believes in him will never perish but experience everlasting life.

John 3:16 (TPT)

If you openly declare that Jesus is Lord and believe in your heart that God raised him from the dead, you will be saved. For it is by believing in your heart that you are made right with God, and it is by openly declaring your faith that you are saved.

Romans 10:9-10 (NLT)

106

PRAYER TO BREAK DEMONIC COVENANTS AND CURSES

Salvation is just the beginning of our life with Jesus Christ. It is the foundation of our belief system. A good foundation requires a clean slate from the former foundations. I recommend reading *Breaking Demonic Covenants and Curses* by Rev. James Solomon, to learn more in depth about this revelational knowledge. I do however want to add in a prayer concerning this! God is a God of covenants and the enemy is a counterfeit. Let's break any and all demonic covenants and curses. Salvation gives us access to Christ's authority that destroys all agreements with darkness. Say this out loud:

In the name of Jesus Christ I repent on behalf of my bloodline from (say whatever comes to mind: i.e perversion, witchcraft, lust, anti marriage, deception,etc).

I renounce all curses connected to the sin of (repeat again, yes be specific as possible because, why not?). I break every demonic covenant made from these sins in my bloodline through acts of my ancestors and my own acts. I break every demonic covenant made through my dreams through eating food, sexual acts and anything unknown to my memory. By the Blood of Jesus Christ, I come out of agreement with all ungodly ties and vows. May the fire of God sever all demonic cycles, covenants, and agreements in my life, in the name of Jesus.

On this day, let Heaven and Earth record that I am in covenant with Jehovah the Most High God, by the Blood of Jesus Christ. I am the righteousness of Jesus Christ and by His grace, His blood is speaking greater things for my life and my bloodline. Who the Son sets free is free indeed. I am free in the name of Jesus Christ and so it shall be.

Now, any and all evil spirits that have been attached to my soul, I evict you now in the name of Jesus Christ. You are in high treason; (Speak out loud any sickness or struggle you have faced, i.e. Arthritis, Cancer, Procrastination, etc) leave me now, and go to a dry place forever!! May the Love of God and His Holy Spirit fill me up until I overflow. In the name of Jesus, Amen.

107

SCRIPTURES

Stand fast therefore in the liberty wherewith Christ hath made us free, and be not entangled again with the yoke of bondage.
   Galatians 5:1 (KJV)

Christ has set us free to live a free life. So take your stand! Never again let anyone put a harness of slavery on you.
   Galatians 5:1 (MSG)

For though we walk in the flesh, we do not war after the flesh: (For the weapons of our warfare are not carnal, but mighty through God to the pulling down of strong holds;)
   2 Corinthians 10:3-4 (KJV)

108

WORSHIP MUSIC I LOVE

Here are a few of my favorite go-to's when I'm praying and championing my day:

STEFFANY GRETZINGER AND HER BESTIE AMANDA COOK

FRED HAMMOND

KARI JOBE

JONATHAN FERGUSON: THE SOUND OF BOOTCAMP (volumes 3 & 4)

BERNARD WILLIAMS, III

NAOMI RAINE

PSALMIST RAINE

109

PRAYER TO RECEIVE BAPTISM OF HOLY SPIRIT

I recommend playing worship music to welcome God into this moment and bring peace into your environment while you pray this out loud:

Father, I repent from a life without Your spirit indwelling on the inside of me. I surrender my all to you. I need Your Power to live this new life.

Let the overflowing power of Your Holy Spirit consume me eternally. By faith I receive You, Holy Spirit, right now! Thank You for baptizing me! Holy Spirit You are welcomed in my life!

Now, relax (take deep breaths, leaving your mouth open enough to speak, YOU CAN NOT STAY SILENT). By faith, begin speaking God's Heavenly language. Speak OUT LOUD. It may sound like small syllables initially, and you may feel awkward, but push past your mind. Your language will grow the more you speak in tongues and you will become more comfortable.

If you prayed this prayer and believed, you can INDEED speak in tongues. This is God's supernatural language! Speak now and every day! It will help you in everything!!!

Stop reading already, and SPEAK OUT LOUD in your new language :)

110

SCRIPTURES

They were all filled and equipped with the Holy Spirit and were inspired to speak in tongues—empowered by the Spirit to speak in languages they had never learned!
Acts 2:4 (NLT)

When someone speaks in tongues, no one understands a word he says, because he's not speaking to people, but to God—he is speaking intimate mysteries in the Spirit.
1 Corinthians 14:2 (TPT)

As he spoke, he showed them the wounds in his hands and his side. They were filled with joy when they saw the Lord! Again he said, "Peace be with you. As the Father has sent me, so I am sending you." Then he breathed on them and said, "Receive the Holy Spirit."
John 20:20-22 (NLT)

Pray in the Spirit at all times and on every occasion. Stay alert and be persistent in your prayers for all believers everywhere.

Ephesians 6:18 (NLT)

About the Author

Shiena is a multi-dimensional, entertainment industry professional and the core of all she does is centered in Jesus Christ.

As Principle of 11:45 ENT, Shiena functions as a Creative Strategist Consultant; skilled in negotiating, client relations and content development for TV/FILM. Her efforts have garnered her solid relationships with TV's major networks and she has become well respected by some of the world's top music directors, executives and musicians. Shiena has worked with or on behalf of: Janelle Monae, Bryan Terrell Clark, Shanice, Mary Mary, Usher, Angie Stone, Deitrick Haddon, Kierra Sheard, PJ Morton, former United States President Barack Obama, Ray Chew Entertainment, and many more.

In the midst of pursuing the entertainment industry, Shiena has continued to serve in ministry. This includes being a lead worshipper in the Arts Department as well as the Executive Administrator/Assistant for Dionny Baez Ministries in Philadelphia, Pennsylvania. During her time there, she was honored to lead worship for bilingual gatherings that streamed live for tens of thousands of people, in several different countries around the world. Her passion was teaching various classes weekly and helping people express their heart to God, through the arts. Prior to, she assisted Sam Collier during his tenure as Musical Director with New Birth Student Ministries in Lithonia, Georgia. In earlier days, she was the Co-Musical Director for her father's church in California.

Refusing to just fit in with the status quo, Shiena is committed to being an answer in mainstream culture and dominating every sector that she works in. With over twenty years of experience, she is ready to pour out all she has learned; making room for continued growth as a budding global media mogul and as a psalmist. Most importantly, Shiena is a daughter of God using her many gifts for people to encounter a tangible presence of His Agapé Love.

Shiena's current projects include The Sound, a live music event, which serves as a spotlight for mental health wellness in the creative community. A compilation of prayers, for the modern day believer of Jesus Christ, *The Heart of the Matter: Volume One, Prayers From Our Hearts to God's Ears* is the first of a trilogy. Shiena's latest single *I Choose You*, is the lead song from her debut album, Loves Vulnerable, and can be heard on all digital outlets, worldwide.

You can connect with me on:
- https://linktr.ee/Shiena
- http://instagram.com/shiena.lene
- http://youtube.com/@ShienaLene

www.ingramcontent.com/pod-product-compliance
Lightning Source LLC
Chambersburg PA
CBHW071356290426
44108CB00014B/1577